Table Of Contents

I am a Gay Man

This book is my interpretation and perspective about being a black gay man finding peace and the creator. I am going to be defining words to help with the understanding of this book.

<u>Gay</u>

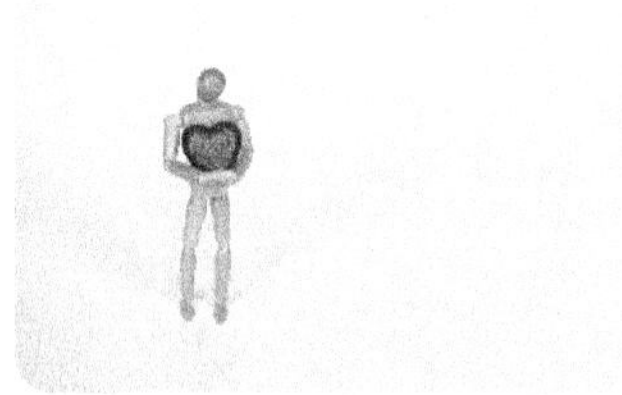

Gay is defined as:

- Relating to or characterized by a sexual or romantic attraction to people of one's same-sex (Merriam-Webster (2021)).

<u>Man</u>

Man is defined as:

•An individual human, especially an adult male human (Merriam-Webster (2021)).

<u>Path</u>

Path is defined as:

•A way of life or thought

•The way or track in which something moves or in which something will be encountered (Merriam-Webster (2021)).

Peace

Peace is defined as:

- Freedom from disquieting or oppressive thoughts or emotions

- Harmony in personal relations

The first step to peace being a gay man is to accept yourself being gay. This may not be easy at first, because other people may not accept that being gay is right.

Therefore, you have to start within yourself and understand that others can not live your life for you. You also have to start a relationship with yourself.

<u>Relationship</u>

The word Relationship is defined as:

•The state of being related or connected (Merriam-Webster (2021)).

I Peace Myself

To start a relationship with yourself, you have to become aware of the thoughts you have about yourself.

Thought

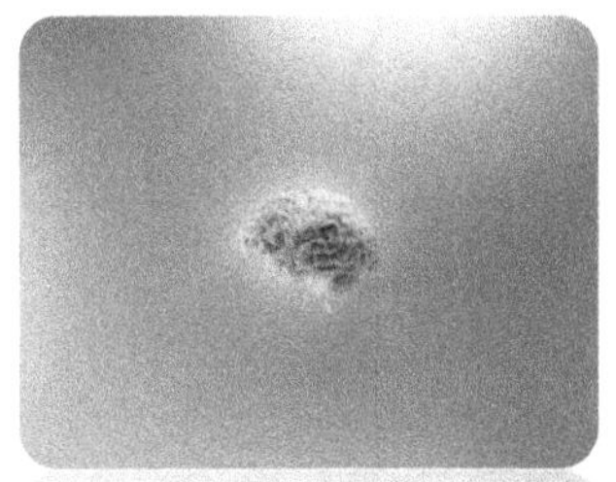

The word thought is defined as:

- An individual act or product of thinking (Merriam-Webster (2021)).

When you are thinking thoughts about yourself, what feeling do you get about yourself?

<u>Feeling</u>

The word feeling is defined as:

• an awareness by your body of something in it or on it: SENSATION (Merriam-Webster (2021)).

Do you feel the sensation of peace? If you feel peaceful then focus on that feeling, believing that is the normal you.

If the answer is no, then think of something that does bring you peace. That feeling is the real you. Understand that peace is our normal state of being and being gay is normal and peaceful.

We have to learn to be at peace with ourselves every day and in every situation of life. It takes practice to maintain peace as gay men

Peace breathing is a breathing exercise we can do whenever we feel overwhelmed, distressed anxiety-filled, or confused.

A lot of us have many situations of life that we wished had never happened to us. These experiences have left us lost, wondering why has this happened to us and thinking nobody cares or understands us.

We think who do we talk to or where do we go for help?

To start you can find a quiet place to be for five minutes. The restroom can work if you cannot find a place to go. When you have found your quiet place, you can begin what is called peace breathing.

•First, sit comfortably on the floor, chair, or just stand.

•Second, close your eyes and concentrate on your breathing.

•Third, breathe in for a count of 1-2-3 and breathe out for a count of 1-2-3.

•Forth, as you breathe in 1-2-3 imagine that the air is the feeling of peace. When you breathe out 1-2-3 imagine peace in the air and it is releasing weight off of your body from the top of the head to the bottom of the feet. Also, relax the body as you breathe out 1-2-3. Do this three times and go back to normal breathing.

•Fifth, once back to normal breathing, stay in the moment and enjoy the presence of peace. Just continue to concentrate on your breathing for about three minutes. If your thoughts stray just bring your focus back to your breathing. Whenever you feel stressed, confused, emotional, worried, or you just want to relax, just do the peace breathing exercise.

Gay Love

Once we have learned peace with ourselves we are ready to have a relationship with our special guy. Understand that same-sex relationships are different than opposite-sex relationships.

Opposite-sex relationships happen because of procreation. Man and women are attracted to each other to have children, which is physical love. Same-sex relationships are not for procreation they express Creator love.

Same-sex relationships transcend the physical and go deeper into the Creator of the person.

Truth

Truth is defined as:

• The body of real things, events, and facts ACTUALITY Merriam Webster (2021)

• Reality and actuality The Free Dictionary (2021)

Creator

The creator is defined as:

- One that creates usually by bringing something new or original into being (Merriam-Webster (2021)).

The creation is defined as:

- Something new that is made or produced: something that has been created (Merriam-Webster (2021)).

Love

Love is defined as

- To like very much (Merriam-Webster (2021)).

We did not create ourselves or the love that we feel for the same sex. The origin place where love comes from is truth. Truth is the idea of how something really is, not what we want it to be, but the way it really is.

Therefore, since we did not create the love we feel for the same sex. Truth is the creator of the love we have, and the creator is love.

Gay love is Creator (truth) love, where the Creator (truth) is expressing love for itself (truth) as a created man. Let me explain:

On the outside of ourselves, there is the weather consisting of:

•Air (Wind)

We need air to breathe, and we did not create the air. That is the truth (Creator), that will not change.

•Water liquid mist (Rain)

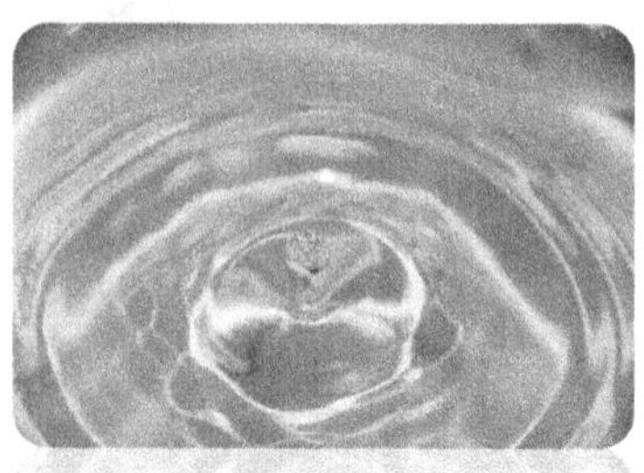

We need to drink water to survive. We did not create water and that is the truth (Creator), that will not change.

•Light, fire, and heat (Sun)

W

e need heat to survive, and we did not create heat ourselves. This is the truth (Creator) that will not change.

Just as the weather is on the outside, it is also on the inside.

Earth, Flesh, and Dust

We need earth as food to eat to survive. We did not create the earth, and this is the truth (Creator), that will not change.

Creation and Body

Our bodies are made of earth, and we are earth vessels for the weather. Just as the earth holds water, our bodies hold water as well. Just like there is air (wind) on the earth, we have the wind in our earth bodies as the breath of life.

<u>Information, Knowledge, and Wisdom</u>

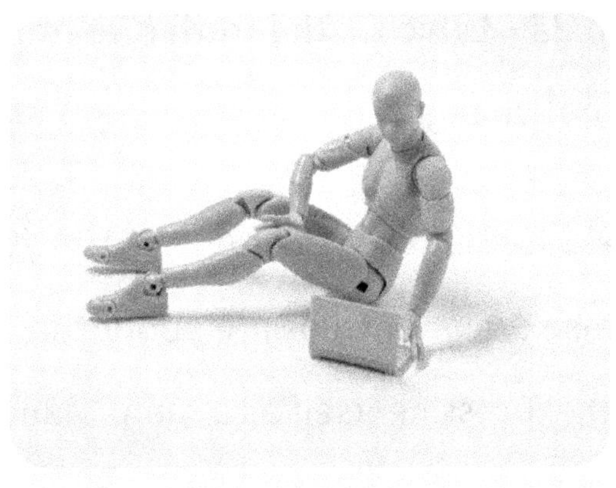

We need the truth (Creator) to survive being:

- Air (wind)

- Water (rain)

- Light and heat (sun)

- Earth (food) and dust

- Creation and body

Which is the information that we survive with each day. Which is the truth (Creator) that will not change.

<u>The Creator of Creation and the Mind of the Body</u>

Since same-sex relationships are about the Creator (truth) expressing itself as a man. Man to man love is the Creator as truthful love. Saying you are the same as me and I love you.

•Mind is defined as being, (the organized conscious and unconscious adaptive mental activity of an organism) Merriam Webster (2021).

Gay love is a pattern of love, where the Creator (truth) and creation (man) are one in the unity of love that brings peace to life.

Gay is Spiritual

Spiritual is defined as:

- of or relating to a person's spirit

- of or relating to religion or religious beliefs

- having similar values and ideas: related or joined in spirit

To be spiritual to me as a gay man is the understanding of the truth being:

•I did not create myself

•Same-sex relationships are different than opposite-sex relationships.

•I have to be at peace with myself before I can be at peace with others.

•Truth is the creator being actually what is.

•Gay love is Creator (truth) love meaning, you are the same as me and I love you. An example is the weather being inside and outside, being one as Creator (truth) and creation (man)

In conclusion, gay is spiritual, manifesting as love and peace with the Creator (truth) and creation (man).

If you are a gay man reading this book. Understand your love is beautiful and you are an expression of the Creator (truth) of creation (man) always and forever in peace.

Thank you for reading.

<u>References</u>

- Merriam-Webster (2021) Gay
Retrieved https://www.merriam-webster.com/dictionary/gay
- Merriam-Webster (2021) Man
Retrieved https://www.merriam-webster.com/dictionary/man
- Merriam-Webster (2021) Path
Retrieved https://www.merriam-webster.com/dictionary/path
- Merriam-Webster (2021) Peace
Retrieved https://www.merriam-webster.com/dictionary/peace
- Merriam-Webster (2021) Relationship
Retrieved https://www.merriam-webster.com/dictionary/relationship
- Merriam-Webster (2021) Thought
Retrieved https://www.merriam-webster.com/dictionary/thought
- Merriam-Webster (2021) feeling
Retrieved https://www.merriam-webster.com/dictionary/feeling
- Merriam-Webster (2021) Truth
Retrieved https://www.merriam-webster.com/dictionary/truth
- Merriam-Webster (2021) Creator
Retrieved https://www.merriam-webster.com/dictionary/creator
- Merriam-Webster (2021) Creation
Retrieved https://www.merriam-webster.com/dictionary/creation
- Merriam-Webster (2021) Love
Retrieved https://www.merriam-webster.com/dictionary/love
- Merriam-Webster (2021) Mind
Retrieved https://www.merriam-webster.com/dictionary/mind
- Merriam-Webster (2021) Spiritual
Retrieved https://www.merriam-webster.com/dictionary/spiritual